OUR QUAKER IDENTITY

Religious society —
or friendly society?

ALASTAIR HERON

Curlew Productions
Kelso, Scotland
1999

Copyright - 1999 Alastair Heron
All rights reserved.

ISBN 1 900259 92 3

Published by Curlew Productions, Thirlestane House, Kelso, Scotland TD5 8PD

Printed by Kelso Graphics, Kelso, Scotland TD5 7BH
Typeset and designed by Curlew Productions, Thirlestane House, Kelso, Scotland TD5 8PD
Cover design by David Woolgrove
Set in New Century Schoolbook 11.4/13.7

'...If it be true that spiritual religion too dimly shines within our borders; if it be true that, in many places, the strength of the bearers of burdens is decayed, it becomes a Christian church not only to acknowledge and deplore the facts, but seriously and in the fear of the Lord to endeavour to ascertain the cause, and to seek for ability to apply the remedy.'[1]

I have no doubt that the Religious Society of Friends (Quakers) in Britain is facing serious difficulties. These are not primarily structural or organisational, but spiritual. The spiritual problems are the direct consequence of changes that began at least thirty years ago, and if nothing effective is initiated soon, in thirty years' time the membership of the Society will need to be described by terms such as ethical, humanist, secular. By then only a minority will affirm personal experience of the living power of the Spirit of God in their daily lives.

I have not come to this conclusion hastily: like others known to me, I have grasped gladly at signs of life, and will continue to do so. No one in his or her right mind seeks a prophetic role, or finds it easy to accept the perception of others that he or she may be 'speaking with a prophetic voice'. This is an essay that I do not want to write: the attempt is being made only because I feel that it is laid upon me to make it. Quakers who know our heritage will recognise that this is what we call a concern.

It is of the essence that this work be set out clearly, in terms that will be as free as possible from ambiguity and equivocation. That will of course sometimes result in an appearance of dogmatism. So let me say right away that I am aware both of that danger, and of 'the possibility that I may be mistaken'. Strictly speaking, the lack of detailed factual knowledge across our nearly 500 local meetings means that hardly any generalisations can validly be made. But for my present task, I cannot avoid making them, however conscious I am that usually there will be exceptions to test the rule. Others have faced this problem before me, both recently and over the last two decades, as I shall record.

In this short non-academic essay, I will try to show that the concern I feel to be laid upon me is well-founded. First, we will look at an earlier critical point in the story of this Yearly Meeting, to learn from it despite the differing pattern of causes, and religious climate. Then I will provide evidence that the present situation has not come suddenly upon us: the signs and symptoms were detected and described at least twenty years ago. These have been confirmed during the decade now ending.

With that as a firm basis, I will address my main task — to focus a light upon some of the principal areas for serious unease at this time. Finally, I shall propose a way forward. That will include some practical action, but it will also be radical in the strict sense of 'going to the root or origin'. Being radical requires us to be honest, to be open, to be both reasonable and courageous. We are never required to assert what we do not believe, but we *are* required to be open to the possibility that through new spiritual experience we will be enabled to believe. I have no easy answers.

I

Just 140 years ago, a 25-year-old Quaker won a hundred guinea prize for his essay[2] on the decline of the Quakers in Britain. He had responded to the following advertisement:

'A gentleman who laments that, notwithstanding the population of the United Kingdom has more than doubled itself in the last fifty years, the Society of Friends is less in number than at the beginning of the century; and who believes that the Society at one time bore a powerful witness to the world concerning some of the errors to which it is most prone, and some of the truths which are the most necessary to it; and that this witness has been gradually becoming more and more feeble, is anxious to obtain light respecting the causes of this change. He offers a prize of One Hundred Guineas for the best essay that shall be written on the subject, and a prize of Fifty Guineas for the one next in merit.'

The advertisement went on to explain that three gentlemen not connected with the Society had agreed to act as adjudicators. The hope was expressed that:

> *'they will choose the one that exhibits most thought and Christian earnestness, whether it is favourable or unfavourable to the Society, whether it refers the diminution of its influence to degeneracy, to something wrong in the original constitution of the body, to the rules which it has adopted for its government, or to any extraneous cause.'*

That signalled recognition that the Society in Britain was seen as being in deep trouble.

The young Quaker was John Stephenson Rowntree, who thirty-six years later conducted the proceedings of 'The 1895 Manchester Conference',[3] an event which initiated what has become known as the 'liberal' era for the Quaker movement in Britain.

Rowntree starts his essay by providing a short account of the circumstances in which the Quaker movement originated, followed by a summary of what he describes as 'Original views of the founders of Quakerism connected with its decline'; this occupies a quarter of his essay. A substantial chapter is then devoted to a review of changes in 'the numerical strength of the Society' between the death of George Fox in 1691 and the year (1859) in which Rowntree was writing.

In the second half of his essay he identifies two further 'epochs': from the death of Fox to the 'revision of the Discipline' in 1760; and the century that followed. Then in a concluding summary chapter he endeavours 'to present, in a condensed form, the causes that appear to have prevented the realisation of those lofty hopes which inspired the bosoms of the 'early Friends'.

John Punshon, in his historical survey *Portrait in grey*[4] observes that:

> 'The impact (of Rowntree's essay) was substantial, and the response of the yearly meeting remarkably prompt. In 1860 the peculiarities (of dress and speech) were made optional, and a year later a complete revision of the discipline was achieved, over fifty rules being removed and participation in the proceedings of yearly meeting was opened to all men members. Legislative approval was obtained, making it possible for non-Quakers to be married in a Quaker meeting.'

It is very obvious that the select membership of the yearly meeting was able to move much more quickly than is possible under our present constitution and procedures.

But Punshon continues:

> *The pace of change after the 1861 Yearly Meeting was slow, as the membership of the Society adapted itself to their internal changes, while becoming slowly aware of external changes that might mean fresh problems to face.'*

These two short quotations serve to highlight the difference, in respect of corporate change, between the purely formal or constitutional, and the spiritual. Rowntree's essay achieved an almost immediate success on the 'constitutional front', but he and others had to work patiently for more than thirty years to see a re-vitalisation of the spiritual life of the Society in Britain.

The causes of decline

John Stephenson Rowntree ended his essay by listing what he perceived to be the set of causes for the decline of the Religious Society of Friends in Britain - the task set by the anonymous donor of the prizes. Let us consider parts of his list.

> *(a) 'In failing fully to discern, or accept, the divinely appointed conditions under which the teachings of the Holy Spirit are ordinarily administered, the founders of Quakerism unconsciously implanted those seeds of decay which - nurtured by successive generations - have borne their natural and destructive fruits.'*

Rowntree had previously made clear his feeling that Fox and early Friends had disparaged the part to be played by human reason, in their concern to emphasise the prior need to rely on the inward leadings of the Holy Spirit. He perceived a lack of balance: I feel the same today, but in recognising the opposite tendency: to doubt or deny the possibility of being inwardly guided, and so to base our reflection and decisions mainly upon our human resources.

> *(b) 'While claiming from the civil powers the utmost liberty of conscience, (the early Friends) did not always allow it to their own followers'.*

This was largely remedied by the 1860 removal of rules about dress and speech, for example. A hundred years later, however, individual Quakers take it for granted that they do have 'the utmost liberty' — not just in matters of conscience, but in almost every other way. Individualism has become the norm.

> *(c) 'Except in the Society's first rise, the gift of religious teaching has been much neglected. The New Testament so fully recognises "teaching" as one of the gifts that no church can neglect its exercise with impunity: and its absence was specially injurious to a body whose public ministry was less intellectual in its character, than that of most other churches.'*

Today the situation is the same: it simply isn't done to provide a 'ministry of teaching', which earns only seven lines in the 1994 *Quaker faith and practice*[5] (2.67). To put it another way, there is no systematic provision of Quaker or biblical teaching: it is left entirely to the individual to take advantage of whatever opportunities for adult religious education may be offered by the meeting or elsewhere. Whether in membership or not, many of those regularly attending meeting for worship can do so for years without learning much about the Quaker heritage of faith.

> *(d) 'Regarding silent waiting on God as one form, and perhaps the highest, in which the adoration of the heart may be offered to Him… the Friends have greatly erred in maintaining it to be the only form of worship which He accepts, and from its being adapted only to certain orders and conditions of mind, the character of public worship, as it is now ordinarily presented in the meetings of the Friends, constitutes an important cause of the fewness of their numbers.'*

In Britain the silence-based meeting for worship, as held usually on Sunday morning, is today sacrosanct — but not wholly for the reason given by Rowntree. It is also what members and regular attenders want and value; for many it proved to be the end of a search, a 'coming home'. They may not feel able to say who or what they have met to worship; their use of the time varies from one person to another; some wish it were wholly silent (as sometimes it is), others tolerate or welcome the spoken ministry provided it is not too predictable or lengthy. But they can reliably be expected to agree that they don't want the form changed — or not much.

> *(e) 'Truly it is only by the help of the Spirit that one "can pray, and pray aright", but when this doctrine has been so urged as to lead persons to expect sensible intimations of its being a duty to pray, instead of finding … the sense of need (a sense begotten by the Holy Spirit), it has occasioned some, through fear of praying amiss, to neglect prayer altogether'.*

Here we come to the first of the two areas in which the differences between 1859 and 1999 are greatest. There are today local meetings in which prayer is offered in the spoken ministry, but it is probably correct to say that this has in general become a rarity. It is not possible to estimate the extent to which individuals engage silently in active prayer, whether of praise, petition or thanksgiving. Spiritual meditation can of course be a 'state of prayer' — probably the purest form of it. But it may not be so: the purpose of meditation varies widely from one person to another.

> f) (about the Bible) '...so jealous in maintaining its inferiority to "the Spirit that gave it forth" ... when the Bible was not read in meetings for worship, nor regularly in the domestic circle, the consequences, by allowing a widespread ignorance of scriptural truth, were most hurtful to the cause of vital religion.'

In 1859 Rowntree could go on thankfully to note that these practices were in fact then returning; but today one has to face a different reality. The reading of the Bible has little or no place in either the meeting for worship or 'the domestic circle'. If it occurs in the former, there is a strong probability that the person involved has grown up and spent many years in one of the mainstream Churches, or is an elderly birthright Quaker. Certainly few newcomers unfamiliar with the Bible (or the New Testament) can expect to remedy that situation by attending a Quaker meeting for worship in Britain. As to 'the domestic circle', it may be said that for all practical purposes the devotional period has disappeared. This may in part be one result of the fact that 'one-Quaker households' are probably now in the majority.

> g) '...during the first half of the eighteenth century ... birthright membership almost imperceptibly established itself. The consequences of this departure from the New Testament idea of a Church have been ... extensive and of serious magnitude'.

It took a further full century for British Quakers to cease the practice of according automatic membership to the children of members, and there are still birthright members scattered through the monthly meetings. Some of these are active in the life of their local meetings, others are but 'names on a list'. (The same may of course be said of many of those who became members 'on personal application' (the term that took the place of 'by convincement').

> *h) 'The renovators of 1760 made hardly any effort to restore the aggressive element to the Society's constitution — their policy was purely defensive; they placed great reliance on penalties, as means for preventing misconduct, and they endeavoured to erect external barriers against the contamination of the world'.*

Here Rowntree is referring to the well-attested fact that early Quakers were evangelists, vigorous 'publishers of Truth'. They were also proselytisers in the correct sense of that term: they sought to draw people away from their existing church allegiances. Many of today's Quakers confuse these terms. It can be said with confidence that British Quakers do not proselytise, but they are (up to a point) active and successful in what they call outreach: our nearly 500 local meetings claim to have about 9000 'recognised Attenders.' But they are strikingly unsuccessful in attracting those attenders into membership.

> *i) 'Within a considerable portion of the present (19th) century, the Society of Friends in England has disowned nearly one-third of all its members who have married, a total of not less than four thousand persons.'*

This was Rowntree's main point, since this accounted for a substantial proportion of the decline in total membership to around 14,000. The discontinuance of disownment for 'marriage before a priest' in 1861 staunched this wound, and progressively ensured an infusion of new blood.

Here it is worth noting that in 1998 only 67 marriages according to Quaker usage took place in meeting houses across Britain. Of these only eight involved two Quakers; in 27 instances, neither party was in membership, the remaining 32 involved one in membership, one not.[6]

Rowntree concludes his essay with an uncompromising challenge:

> 'Let the present leaders of the Society, and let every serious and reflective Friend, be assured that talking about its decline, and "paraphrasing the causes of it", under sentences which do but mislead, will avail nothing. The consciousness of personal integrity and of earnest self-denying labour, will not atone for want of knowledge, or for inadequate or timorous measures. The crisis is far too solemn in its character to permit of trifling'.

I have no hesitation in identifying myself with Rowntree's forthrightness in our present situation.

Overview

Quakers in Britain were numerically at their lowest ebb when Rowntree wrote his essay. They were also divided, though spared the painful formal separations that had riven Quakers in the USA in the 1820s. In Britain, those of an evangelical persuasion still went to the silence-based meeting for worship along with those perceived as conservatives. As we have noted, in 1860 the yearly meeting was united in taking prompt action in response to the essay.

But unlike the situation that prevails today, they had no doubt that they were a religious body, and a Christian one at that, albeit of a distinctive kind. Those of a conservative persuasion continued to emphasise the distinctive features, but those affirming an evangelical position were doctrinally somewhat difficult to distinguish from those in membership of mainstream Christian churches. Unlike their counterparts in the USA, British Quakers continued to depend upon their unpaid, recorded ministers, and did not employ pastors.

The relevance for us today of the situation in 1859 — what we have in common despite the manifest differences — is the urgent need to recognise that we are in trouble, and to seek appropriate ways of rising out of it.

II

If one is deeply concerned about something, those who do not share that feeling can too easily be perceived as complacent — as being contented and satisfied when they ought not to be! That simply won't do: whether someone is satisfied or not depends on their expectations. So it is more accurate to judge that expectations are low, than to talk about complacency. In the present matter, that leads one to wonder what most Quakers in Britain actually expect from the religious society of which they are members.

Here I must hazard what I hope will be an informed guess. A start can be made by saying confidently that the majority of them would like to be provided with a 'good' meeting for worship on Sunday mornings. 'Good' means some spoken ministry, not too long, not too solemn, and not from the same people most weeks. It may also mean encouraging, comforting, sometimes even mildly uplifting. Most will not actively expect an overtly religious content, reference to the Bible, or vocal prayer.

There is likely to be an expectation that in times of personal or domestic trouble help will be available, both informally and through the overseers. Only a minority will expect to be provided regularly or frequently with opportunities for learning about the Quaker heritage, or for widening and deepening their spiritual life, or that of their meeting. When such opportunities are provided, most will not feel a need to make use of them, or will accord them low priority in the use of their disposable free time.

In many smaller or isolated meetings, it may be difficult to meet even these modest expectations, and members may be far from content, realistically making the best of what they have. On the other hand there are certainly similarly-placed meetings where such expectations are met more fully than in some larger meetings around the country. Again I must make clear how very aware I am of the many ways in which both the situation and the climate of meetings can and do vary.

But I think that overall it is likely that, across the yearly meeting, there is a generally low level of expectation among the members of our local meetings on matters of spiritual depth. But in many meetings a minority of more active members have expressed their anxieties, and have taken opportunities to seek for help.

I have not been alone in these perceptions. Yearly Meeting in May 1998 accepted the report of the Memorandum Group on Constitutional Review. The concluding statement of that report[7] opened with the following :

> '*Spiritual renewal and constitutional review.*
>
> *The consultations we have undertaken, formally through Monthly Meetings between January and May 1997, and less formally through two open meetings at Yearly Meeting 1997, have confirmed our consistent impression that what Friends are seeking, not least in their meetings for church affairs, is spiritual renewal. The relevance of constitutional change to this continuing search remains unclear to many Friends, though crystal clear to some. As we minuted on 28 September 1997:*
>
> *"The spiritual state of the Society continues to be emphasised as the object of Friends' dissatisfaction."*

And the oral summary presented by the Clerk of the Memorandum Group ended with these words:

> *Spiritual renewal is what Friends are after, and that is where the emphasis should lie. A spiritually-renewed Britain Yearly Meeting will be better-placed, when the time is ripe, to devote resources to constitutional review.'* **(His emphasis)**

Let me repeat: although many *individual* members active in the life of the Society, whether locally, in their monthly meeting, or through central channels, are uneasy about our corporate spiritual health, the majority must be assumed to be largely content with things as they are. The validity of this distinction is inherent in the generally low attendance at meetings for worship for business, and a consequent readiness to let things carry on largely unchanged. The fact has to be faced that reports or statements from monthly meetings may represent only the perceptions of a dedicated minority, except when special arrangements are made to involve many more members in detailed consideration of a key issue or topic.

Earlier alerts

During the last two decades there have been several attempts to evaluate the Quaker situation in Britain. Extracts from these will serve to illuminate the evolution of our current difficulties.

In 1980 Woodbrooke College published an essay written by Joan Fitch, who had spent the previous session there, as the holder of what was then known as a Fellowship (now Friend in Residence). In this essay, entitled *The present tense*,[8] she...

> '*made an attempt to find out why present-day Quakers seem unable to state our faith convincingly to the world, just at a time when it is so desperately needed. In making*

this attempt, I have written, sometimes very personally, from my own experience, as it seemed wrong to ask others to be articulate about their faith if I were not prepared to be so myself where it was relevant. I have revealed some of my misgivings about the present state of the Society of Friends in this country. Sometimes I have suggested changes which may or may not commend themselves to Friends,'

In her first chapter, on 'The situation today', she observes:

*'I think it fair to say that the enquirer in a Quaker Meeting today will be lucky if, over several weeks, he or she hears any Friend refer in ministry to outspoken specific matters of faith or belief, and that **the main drift of what is said will be of a liberal, kindly, non-committal sentiment**' (p.3)* (**My emphasis**)

Then in 'The contemporary scene' we have:

*'The Quaker conception of the spiritual life is threefold: the personal, direct experience of God; the struggle to express and understand the experience; and the acting-out of inspiration in terms of living. I would say that Friends were originally strong on all three emphases, but that **nowadays the middle strand is almost missing**.' (p.10)* (**My emphasis**)

And under 'The Quakers: present'

'How do I see the Society of Friends here and now? I see us as a small body: quiet, sober, respected, ageing, middle-class, compassionate, incorruptible, usually liberal but rarely radical.' (p.21)

Her essay was realistic but not negative: she challenged British Quakers to address their spiritual needs, personally and corporately. The essay sold well, requiring a reprint in 1981, and was certainly used by study groups in meetings around Britain. But the overall response may be gauged by what I have observed elsewhere about Yearly Meeting 1981: 'British Quakers welcomed the opportunity to be comfortable, and to enjoy an uneventful yearly meeting'.

In between

One evening during the 1995 Summer Gathering held at the University of Lancaster, I gave an address partly based on points raised in the final chapter of a book[9] published on the first day of the Gathering. Most of them seem appropriate at this juncture:

> *(a) Quakers in Britain are still searching for a new identity in a 'post-liberal' era already 30 years old. At the very beginning of that era the American Quaker scholar Hugh Barbour wrote of Quakers in Britain:*
>
>> *'They are not agreed upon the aims which they ought corporately to be pursuing, and consequently are in danger either of simultaneously pursuing mutually incompatible aims, or of settling for the view that the Society's aim must be to support and encourage impartially its members in the pursuit of their individual aims …By default, the latter alternative has prevailed.'–*
>
> *(b) While officially a Christian body, it may already be the case that only a minority of its members would describe themselves as Quaker Christians.*
>
> *(c) Total membership is at best static, mainly because only a tiny fraction of those who fairly regularly attend a Quaker meeting, and take part in its social life as well as in the weekly meeting for worship, see any need to*

commit themselves to formal membership. Both attenders and recent new members report as another factor, the general tendency of members to be perennial seekers, unable or unwilling to share their spiritual findings in a convincing way.

(d) Although the monthly meetings are the basic units of the Quaker structure, and as such have total responsibility for all aspects of membership, they are nominally preserved from anarchy by the Book of Christian discipline *as accepted by Britain Yearly Meeting. But it has been shown that they tend to treat the 'church government' provisions of that Book mainly as guidelines, because they understand that nothing is 'laid upon them as a rule or form to walk by'.*

(e) Many British Quakers focus their interest and active participation upon the local meeting which they attend regularly, and have little or no interest in the 'central' life and work of the yearly meeting as a whole. Partly as a result of this, some meetings display a 'congregational' attitude.

(f) Monthly meetings for worship for business are very poorly attended: this trend increased as new members have for many years been inadequately prepared for their responsibilities. Monthly meeting boundaries unrelated to modern demography and transport are another relevant factor.

(g) The admitted 'wide diversity of belief' within the membership makes it uncertain what proportion of those who do take part in business meetings share the intention to 'seek the will of God' in making decisions on matters of substance.

(h) In the absence of a paid clergy, Quakers in Britain carry a shared responsibility for all aspects of the

administration and nurture of their meetings, at every 'level' and of their members and frequent attenders. Modern social and employment conditions combine to prevent an even distribution of these responsibilities across the adult age-range and as between women and men.

(i) Judging by the 1992 intake of new members the average age of the membership is increasing, as is the proportion of women, currently three to every two men. This proportion is not however reflected in the most responsible positions of service in the Yearly Meeting which are held largely by women Friends.

Some of these points echo those made by Joan Fitch fifteen years earlier, others had also been raised in articles and correspondence in *The Friend* and other Quaker periodicals, and in Woodbrooke and other conferences and study meetings. The study which gave rise to them was among others drawn upon by the author of the 1997 Swarthmore Lecture.

The 1997 Swarthmore Lecture

This was given under the title *Previous convictions* [10] by Christine Trevett, seventeen years a Quaker, during the residential Yearly Meeting in Aberystwyth. It is accurately described on the back cover as 'a very personal look at the late twentieth-century Religious Society of Friends (which) comments on the effects of increased liberalism, individualism, and the "culture of silence" when trying to consider the transmission of Quaker faith and values.' (The qualification 'in Britain' should have appeared after 'Religious Society of Friends': ours is but one of the many yearly meetings in the 'world family of Friends', several of which list much larger memberships).

Christine Trevett drew upon several other recently-published historical and sociological studies of British Quakers, to broaden the base of her evaluation, as well as upon her own spiritual journey and her theological training. For our immediate purpose, here are some quotations from the published lecture:

> 'As I pondered the matter of writing about transmission of faith, I found myself asking more urgently **whether Quakerism knew what it was.** How were those of us who were in it to determine whether the seeker was finding, or whether the road to finding was recognisably a Quaker one? Or were such questions now without meaning? Dared we any longer speak of well- trodden paths and of assured guidance for those who are open to it? Were some meetings refusing to offer signposts, even declaring that they were redundant?' (p.30-31) (**My emphasis**)

> 'All kinds of models of Quakerism are in the air. For myself, I continue to believe that Quakerism is something, is a religious Society and that we may jeopardise it if we assume too readily that anything and everything can be embraced within its motherly arms without extending these too far for well-being.' (p.90)

> 'From the days of Mary Fisher and William Penn, Robert Barclay and John Woolman, we can find witnesses to Friends' openness to 'the promptings of truth and love' as evidenced in the hearts of people quite different from themselves. We can find from those times a Quaker view of the 'catholic' (=universal) Church which speaks of a commonality of inward transformation such as may be found among peoples of all faiths. This is different from Catholic allegiance to doctrines of apostolic succession or the need for ordained male hierarchies. One does not have to carry a label such as 'Quaker universalist' to continue to hold to such truths.

> But recognising the universal applicability of Quaker truths is one thing. It is surely not the same as assuming that Quakerism becomes no less Quakerism, is unchanged or improved, by selected and diluted additions of truths characteristic of Buddhism, Sufism, Adlerian psychology, native American Indian theology or whatever, and to varying degrees from Meeting to Meeting, Friend to Friend. Being informed by is quite different from being conformed to, or seeking to conform Quakerism to such things.
>
> Here I stand.
>
> 'Quakerism, I dare to say (and it will not make me popular amongst a considerable number of Friends) is not Buddhism, transactional analysis (or is that passé now?) or synonymous with the world view of the Labour Party (of which I am a member). It is not a less demanding substitute for Judaism though it is where many Friends can take a "Jewish" unitarian stance. I may well have gained from the insights of such religions from time to time, but I do not live the life (life, and "in the Life", not "lifestyle") of them. If I did, then would I not be a Buddhist or a Jew? Evidently I am not a person who believes of the world's religious traditions that "we all believe the same things really". No we don't, though we may certainly learn from one another.' (p.91)

And then she grasps the nettle firmly —

> 'But if there is any agreement worth a mention about what we stand for, then I think we must stand for it. **We must ensure that it is understood by those who wish to be part of us and are part of us.** This is not credalism. This is taking seriously the validity of our corporate leadings, and the experience of our history.' (p.144) (**My emphasis**)

As Christine Trevett noted, her analysis of the current health of Britain Yearly Meeting would not endear her to many of those who had exercised their right to take part in the 1997 yearly meeting. A similar fate may have befallen both John Punshon's Lecture in 1992 (*Testimony and tradition*), and that of Margaret Heathfield in 1994 (*Being together*). Many British Quakers are liable these days to be made restive by such passages as the following:

(from *Testimony and tradition*)[11]:

> 'In contrast to this image of a tree with all its different parts integrally related, I sometimes think that what we have nowadays is more like a supermarket. One may wander round the Friendly emporium selecting from the shelves whatever nourishment one chooses, with very little restriction. The tins and packets in the trolley do not need to add up to a consistent or balanced diet. Such items are related not by their inherent properties, but by the conscious choice of the purchaser. Thus the activist may have one shopping list, the contemplative another. Supermarket Quakerism can dispense with the idea that the testimonies are each part of a greater whole, from which they derive their cogency, and that there is a basis for them which is not necessarily sympathetic to the presuppositions of rationalism and humanism.' (p. 23)

(from *Being together*)[12]:

> 'Is our Yearly Meeting a People of God, able to speak with one voice and expressing heavenly harmony, or are we a religious movement which supports our individual journeys wherever they lead?' (p.108)

Were it possible to pose those alternative roles for our yearly meeting to an adequate representative sample of BYM members, I do not doubt a clear majority for the latter, even though an unknown number would abstain because of the term 'religious'.

Recent evidence of disquiet

Since the 1998 Yearly Meeting, in addition to a number of relevant letters and articles in *The Friend*, the spiritual health of the yearly meeting has exercised both the Central Committee of Quaker Home Service, and its Committee on Eldership and Oversight. Extracts from the minutes of the Committee on Eldership and Oversight for its meetings in June and August 1998 contain the following passages:

> *'In preparation for Yearly Meeting 1999 we will communicate through QHS Central Committee the need for an exploration of spiritual learning and nurture within the Yearly Meeting. We will also submit a paper direct to YM Agenda Committee.'* (13.6.98)

> *The suggestion is a session of Yearly Meeting 1999 on spiritual nurture, within an overall Yearly Meeting theme of spirituality within Britain Yearly Meeting.'* (12/13.8.98) (**My emphasis**)

And in the minutes of QHS Central Committee we find:

*'The expression of spiritual hunger and the need for exploring ways of spiritual nurture have been brought to us by members of Central Committee, and we agree that the time is right for this to be brought as a major concern to YM Agenda Committee. We are glad that this issue is being **addressed by the Committee on Eldership and Oversight...**'.* (18.7.98) (**My emphasis**)

In the event, Y.M. Agenda Committee decided 'we will not be discussing spiritual nurture, but will be actively feeding and nurturing ourselves and one another, hopefully equipping ourselves with resources we can take back to our home Meetings, as George Fox put it, "awakening the witness."' Perhaps the key word in that passage from Documents in Advance is 'hopefully'.

A session of Yearly Meeting is however, being devoted to 'trusting our discernment', particularly in relation to the corporate decision-making of the Yearly Meeting.

Overview

Clearly I have been selective in the interests of brevity: I could have started earlier than 1980, and I could have drawn upon a much wider range of evidence. But now is the time to emphasise that the composite picture just presented has remained consistent over the last twenty years in spite of the strenuous efforts made to address the problems. Both Quaker Home Service and Woodbrooke College, separately and in cooperation, have striven to provide materials and opportunities. Notable among these efforts are the 'Gifts and discoveries' and the 'Resources for learning' programmes.
Individual members and attenders have taken advantage of these offerings, and have made clear their appreciation. In some cases individual gains have also benefited local meetings. But we are still talking of a minority, and we do not know how to evaluate the spiritual benefits.

In the next section I will marshal some of my own perceptions, and try to achieve a clear picture of the present situation.

III

We have seen how over the past twenty years concern has frequently been clearly expressed about the spiritual health of what we now know as Britain Yearly Meeting. This may be thought of collectively as prophecy, using that term in the religious sense of inspired awareness.

It is fair to say that, on the part of the majority of our membership, little or no sustained heed has been given to any of these insights, or to their cumulative import for Quakers in Britain. The deteriorating process has consequently continued unchecked, not even by the exercises, involving many Quakers in their local meetings, that resulted in the adoption of *Quaker faith and practice* by the 1994 Yearly Meeting, as what we call our 'Book of Christian discipline'.

In this section, I will first focus on three areas of concern — membership; eldership and oversight; the relation between members in their local meetings and what are usually referred to as 'central bodies'. Then I shall consider three key words in the title and sub-title of the 1994 *Quaker faith and practice*, the 'red book' that lies on many meeting house tables during Meeting for Worship on Sunday mornings — our 1999 preferred book of reference, not always accompanied by a copy of the Bible.

Finally, against that background, attention will be directed to our local meetings.

Membership

Unlike John Stephenson Rowntree in 1859, responding to the anonymous donor of the prizes, my concern is not focused on the slowly falling membership of the yearly meeting. The question must however be addressed, and in a way appropriate to our present situation. We claim to have about 17,000 adult members and over 9000 fairly regular attenders. I have good reason to think that both those figures are seriously inflated. In most of our local meetings, substantial numbers of members do not wish to resign or to have their membership terminated by the monthly meeting, even though they seldom or never come to meeting for worship, and are not involved in the life of the meeting, except perhaps financially.

In January 1999 the convenors of overseers in six of our ten largest Meetings provided estimates of the number of their listed members 'likely to be seen at meeting for worship at least twice a month'. Their estimates ranged from 33 to 45 per cent, averaging 41 per cent of the 1048 listed as members of the six Meetings.

Inflation of the figures for attenders arises from the flexibility exercised by overseers in their use (if referred to) of the definition of an attender in *Quaker faith and practice* (11.45) as 'one who, not being a member, frequently attends a specific meeting for worship'. Is about once a month 'frequently'? So for practical purposes, as well as a matter of integrity, I suggest that we see ourselves as having about 10.000 fairly active members, and about 5,000 fairly frequent attenders. For a 'do it yourself' body scattered over the whole of Britain, and supporting a hierarchical structure of business meetings as well as a central organisation, that is not many. More serious however is the fact that there are only two members for each attender; and, more serious still, that only about 300 attenders become members in any one year.

There are quite a few British Quakers who think that we should simply abolish membership, and let anyone claim to be a Quaker who wishes to do so. This, they say, would remove the problem that even those attenders who take an active part in the life of the meeting, and may have done so for many years, are precluded from service as clerks, elders, overseers and treasurers, and should not be appointed as Quaker representatives on outside bodies. To these Friends my considered response continues to be that which I made in *Now we are Quakers*[13] (p.53), where I observed:

> *'As a religious body without paid clergy, the Yearly Meeting cannot differ from any other corporate body: responsibility for effective realisation of its avowed purposes is vested in those who have accepted a formal commitment to promote those purposes. Only those — in a commercial cooperative society, a professional association, or a religious body — who are perceived publicly as committed members, can or should speak in the name of that society, association or body.*
>
> *However much any of us may wish, as some have said and written that they do, for an ideal situation in which "membership" could be abolished, so that anyone could say that he or she was "a Quaker" when they felt personally free to do so, it is not a practical proposition, and it will be in everyone's best interests — and that of our Quaker body — to recognise this'.*

We know that some meetings have experienced considerable difficulty in identifying members suitable and willing to serve as clerks, treasurers, elders or overseers. The task of nomination committees has become increasingly difficult, despite the belated but welcome recognition that it is not 'un-Quakerly' to express an interest in a particular service, provided one takes no umbrage if the offer does not result in nomination.

There is a marked shortage of men, their total numbers having fallen by nearly 1100 between 1977 and 1997[14]. In 1992, more than half the new members, across the yearly meeting, were over 50 years of age, so we are also an ageing society. Unlike in 1859, we cannot be rejuvenated by a steady intake of young adult birthright members.

Eldership and oversight

The changes that have taken place over the past twenty years have been adverse to a ministry that is vital in a 'church without a clergy'. Yes — we are all 'priests' in a 'priesthood of all believers', but we lay additional responsibilities for a time on some of our number. The lower the proportion of 'believers', the heavier do those responsibilities become.

Eleven years ago the then 'Yearly Meeting Executives' of elders and of overseers jointly issued a report[15], based on information obtained from a postal survey addressed to convenors of elders and overseers in all our meetings. It was hoped that the report would be used as the basis for discussion about the needs of those we ask to provide eldership and oversight, and how some of these needs might be met.

The survey questionnaire containing twenty-eight questions was sent to 788 MM and local meeting conveners, 514 of whom responded: an encouraging result, especially since on several criteria it was fully representative. Here is the summary of the report:

> 'It can fairly be said that the information obtained from this survey did make a useful contribution to our firm knowledge about the problems faced at that time by those on whom we lay the burden of providing eldership and oversight. Unlike many surveys, it did not merely tell us what we knew already, though it may have provided evidence for what some Friends had suspected to be the case.
>
> ...the response supports some anecdotal evidence about increasing need for more elders and overseers, or else for a range of alternative models for more effective provision. It seems reasonable to relate this to the large and growing numbers of attenders and enquirers in very many meetings, as well as to the spiritual and other difficulties faced by those already in membership. A substantial minority of meetings have apparently given some consideration to alternative modes of provision, and several have gained experience in experimenting with these.
>
> Even making full allowance for proper restraint in the use of descriptive terms, especially of a 'religious' nature, one cannot avoid being struck by the fact that **only 26 of over 700 responses mentioned 'spiritual experience' as one of the "main strengths" of elders and overseers.** It is therefore not surprising that almost all the convenors felt 'ill-equipped' for their roles; that a quarter of their answers were explicit about 'lack of confidence' or 'feeling inadequate'; or that a further quarter referred to lacks in 'sensitivity' or 'spirituality', and of 'theological and/or practical knowledge'. In a religious society which is explicitly based and dependent for its vitality on first-hand personal and communal experience of the Inward Light at work in

us, the implications of these responses surely call for exploration, by other means but still on a wide front.

It is encouraging that half the answers to the question, 'How do you nurture yourself spiritually?' referred to reading, Bible study, prayer, meditation and times of quiet. But we need to know with what success they turned to 'Friends in the meeting' for pastoral or spiritual help, as nearly half said they did. Encouragement for the idea of providing systematic help or training on first being appointed an elder or overseer was forthcoming from three-quarters of the convenors: with an average of nine years service already behind them, it was hardly surprising that many fewer saw any point in suggesting what might be 'desirable now'. Finally, there seems to be some spontaneous expression of a need to rescue the roles — perhaps especially that of elder — from past associations of an 'elitist' nature. For a peace-loving people, present-day Friends can be fiercely egalitarian and individualistic. They are certainly in a contemporary muddle about the nature of freedom and authority, and of an acceptable relation between these. Be that as it may, it must be recognised as relevant in any attempt to make plans, or to bring about structural changes, aimed at strengthening and making more effective our provision of eldership and oversight in our meetings.' **(My emphasis)**

Ten years ago this was a deeply disturbing picture. There is no compelling reason to think that it has improved: on the contrary, we are probably now still further away from William Dewsbury's 1653 proposal that each meeting should appoint 'one or two most grown in the Power and the Life, in the pure discerning of the Truth, to take responsibility for the spiritual welfare of the meeting and its members'. In modern usage, the word 'elder' has no necessary connection with chronological age; but only one generation ago it certainly implied 'a seasoned Friend', regardless of age.

If as seems likely there is a shortage of such 'seasoned Friends' in some monthly meetings, it may be necessary to follow the advice set out in *Quaker faith and practice* (3.23):

> *'It is generally undesirable for someone to hold an appointment for more than six years continuously, although there may be exceptions'.* (**My emphasis**)

Central funding and congregational tendencies

Within the provisions of our present constitution, we have addressed vigorously the problems arising from financial stringency, and as part of that activity have tried to make our administrative and policy-making processes more efficient. We have reduced the staff of our central departments and are moving towards the amalgamation of two of them. Quaker Home Service, the department entrusted with 'sustaining the fabric of Quaker life, deepening the spiritual life of Friends and meetings, and promoting outreach at local and national level', is now seriously under-resourced for such responsibilities. For example, its Literature Committee was 'saddened to learn that the post of literature editor was to disappear at the end of 1998', noting that this had 'serious implications for the work of the Committee, bearing in mind the inevitable additional pressures on the already stressed and overworked Friends House staff'.

Although there have been substantial short-term responses to appeals for more giving to central work, it remains clear that very many British Quakers do not identify themselves with it, and may prefer to support their local meeting. In a survey[16] which attracted a sixty per cent response from those across the yearly meeting who had become members during 1992, two-thirds felt very little or no involvement with 'central work'. There is also some evidence[17] that many British Quakers channel significant proportions of their disposable money and time to non-Quaker charitable bodies, such as Oxfam, Amnesty International, Christian Aid, Shelter and many others. It has rightly been observed that one of the main sources of central funds — legacies — is almost certain to shrink, as more people live longer and therefore use their money to make provision for residential and nursing care in their later years. Account must also be taken — both locally and nationally — of the fact that (as we have noted) many members today live in a 'one Quaker household'; and also, to extents probably varying widely from meeting to meeting, a 'single parent household'. In the former case, available funds are unlikely to go wholly towards Quaker needs; in the latter case, little or nothing may be available at all.

Such considerations also apply to the readiness of members to take part in events, such as the four-yearly residential yearly meetings, and Summer Gatherings, the cost of which have soared well beyond the reach of all but the markedly better off (despite bursary help). So far as the yearly meeting occasions are concerned, this means that participation in the business of the residential Yearly Meetings is becoming progressively unrepresentative of the active membership.

From all this it is difficult to avoid the conclusion that Quaker life in Britain will increasingly become focused on the local meeting. Given a general absence of signs that involvement in the business of monthly meetings is on the increase, 'local' means what it says. Britain Yearly Meeting is well on the way to becoming a mainly congregational body.

'Religious' and 'discipline'

At the close of the two-part Yearly Meeting in 1994, there were very mixed feelings abroad around Britain. While thankfulness was expressed that 'we have a book', many indicated their recognition that it reveals the extent to which the continuity of our Quaker Christian heritage was becoming tenuous. That was tacitly acknowledged when the Yearly Meeting changed from 'Christian' to 'Quaker' in the main title — against the recommendation of the Review Committee — while retaining 'Christian' in the sub-title. I shall address this question a little later.

But at that time it was also felt right to retain the word 'Religious' in the title of the yearly meeting. I have addressed this question elsewhere[18] in the following terms:

> *'Is our name 'The Religious Society of Friends (Quakers) in Britain' an accurate description?'*

to which in 1995 I answered:

> *'I think it is. There are certainly members scattered all over the yearly meeting who would prefer to drop the word 'religious' from the title, and many others who are very little bothered by the frequency with which it is dropped, whether on the notice-boards outside Quaker meeting houses; in articles to* The Friend *and other Quaker periodicals; or even in the minutes of their preparative or monthly meeting.*
>
> *But probably most Quakers in Britain would wish their membership to be perceived as of 'a religious body'. Whatever they may make individually of what they do in the meeting for worship, or to what or to whom the worship is being addressed, they know intuitively that it is at least intended to be something more than an*

> *occasion for individual and group meditation. And — unless they have been unfortunate, perhaps through long years in the same local meeting without much depth of spiritual life — they will have known occasions when the meeting for worship was special: some of the others present may have called it 'gathered' or, more rarely, 'covered'.*
>
> *This does not mean, however, that a growing individualism has not made possible some degree of secularism. In a warm, sustaining atmosphere of what attenders unite in acclaiming as a combination of "acceptance, friendliness and tolerance", it is easy to let a meeting become a social club, largely run by the members but for the benefit of all who come to meeting.'*

In the four years that have passed since that was written, there have been indications of further movement in that direction: a secular or humanist trend reflects a growing lack of personal spiritual experience. More individual Quakers are ready to say outright that they have no belief in God, to doubt whether they 'worship' in meetings dedicated to that purpose.

I also asked the question 'Should it be called a book of discipline?', and went on:

> 'We have adequate evidence that Quakers in Britain today are in general so individualistic that they have difficulty with terms like authority, leadership and discipline. Insofar as they try to follow the leadings of whatever 'the inner light' (or 'the Inner Light') means for them ...this is perhaps understandable. But we know that the danger lies in perceiving individual leadings as reliable without the 'checking' of the worshipping group. That checking is not common practice today.'

This is in sharp contrast to the words used in a yearly meeting minute during the 1967 revision of what was then *Church government*:

> *Our church government is not a government of sanctions, but the attempt to express the leadings — and also the disciplines — of the Holy Spirit in our life as a community,* and as we deal with our day-to-day administrative affairs. (**My emphasis**)

I went on to say that I believed

> '*our continued use of the ecclesiastical term "discipline" in the domain of what was until now 'church government', is misleading because it does not represent our corporate practice. Apart from the legal requirements in relation to marriage,* **there are almost no rules**. *Monthly meetings and individuals are being offered only guidelines that corporately the Yearly Meeting in session has felt to be appropriate. Very little appears to be intended as* prescriptive. (**My emphasis**)

It has been shown conclusively[19] that current practice in monthly and preparative meetings reflects an assumed permissiveness. More seriously, many British Quakers have gone on record as questioning or rejecting the very basis of our way of conducting business — that in reaching decisions on matters of substance we are actively seeking to perceive the purposes of God.

'Christian'

Although it is not my purpose in this book to engage in 'special pleading' for a return to our Christian heritage, a picture of the present scene would be incomplete without some consideration of this issue.

In the report of the working party that in 1986 produced *The nature and variety of concern*[20], this appears:

> *'It still seems widely acceptable to describe ourselves — and to welcome new members — as "humble learners in the school of Christ". This is fast becoming a Quaker cliché. Are its implications usually apparent to those who use it? How do we learn, and how is our learning guided? Do most Friends see themselves as disciples, because they sit at the feet of one who can still teach his people himself? Or do most of our problems in the area of concern arise from our lack of a personal faith, based on our living experience, in a living spirit which can teach us, call us, empower us?'* (pp 14-15)

I think we must look more closely at the fact of our Christian heritage, and what it means to Friends today. I can describe it as the fact because the evidence is so clear that nobody seems to question it. But it is also a fact that during the last 25 to 30 years an increasing number of those in membership of unprogrammed Quaker meetings around the world have become hesitant about describing themselves as Christians. Of that number there are many who go further and express themselves as unable to do so. In such a process of institutional change there are bound to be many strands of causation, from which any attempt at selection must to some extent be arbitrary: I shall focus on but three.

Acceptance into membership of sincere recruits who made no pretence to any personal convictions of a Christian character, however loosely defined; frequently had acquired but little knowledge of our history or understanding of our religious practices and their basis; and perceived the Society primarily as an active agent of protest, most notably in the peace, anti-nuclear, social action and environmental movements.

The second strand can be thought of in terms of a progressive loss of personal conviction on the part of established members of our religious society who had, earlier in their lives, gladly seen themselves as 'humble learners in the school of Christ'

The third is the growth of a climate in which there has been a widespread rejection of religious language, which has resulted in major problems of communication. It has become steadily more difficult to speak about one's faith, the more so when there is no credal statement or accepted body of doctrine to which reference can be made by way of explanation. Our corporate response to the World Council of Churches in *To Lima with love* [21] is the nearest thing we have to such a point of reference, but some of its content is unacceptable to many British Quakers.

Taken together, these three strands are more than adequate to account for the great increase in diversity among us; for the difficulties now faced when we try to reach a fresh understanding of the meaning of membership; for a significant secular trend among a company of people famous for their conviction that all life is sacramental; and most important of all, for the widespread and growing inability to tell one another of what our faith consists.

Towards a diagnosis

In this section we have been facing some of the more salient facts of our present situation. Let us act now like a sympathetic physician, who considers both 'signs' (what is observable) and 'symptoms' (what is experienced). Most of what we considered in this section may be regarded as 'signs', To these we can add — the number and variety of 'listed interest groups' [22] which are concerned with explicitly spiritual issues. Their founders and members offer a common explanation for their existence as groups: the lack of fellowship, encouragement and channels of expression within the local and regional structure, with a resulting need for some 'nationwide' forum and meeting point. A second sign, associated with this, is the growing disquiet about the balance between the 'local' and 'central' origins of distinctively Quaker initiatives, and about our considerable reliance upon the recruitment of non-Friends as workers in 'Quaker' projects, rather than on Friends who have experienced a 'concern' and have been 'released' (that is, recognised and enabled) to carry it out themselves.

A third sign is the increased tendency to 'label' ourselves and one another, and then to use the labels in ways that tend to be divisive. This may be related to a fourth sign, the most disturbing of all: the clear evidence of unloving intolerance, displayed in such behaviour as public reproach for the use of familiar religious language by individual members or attenders in their vocal ministry. Fifth, as we have noted, there are reports of increasing difficulty in finding Friends with the spiritual gifts appropriate to the ministries of eldership. And finally, in a list clearly not exhaustive, we have also noted that, while enjoying the interest and presence of many thousands of attenders, we can record only a tiny handful becoming members each year. Is there already a thoughtful look on the face of the physician'?

What about symptoms? A survey[23] some years ago in a large urban meeting, reporting what people did when taking part in the meeting for worship, showed that only about half the twenty-seven respondents made some reference to God, Spirit or Presence, very few of these to praise, thanksgiving or prayer. Elsewhere, many of those

37

usually taking part in their local meeting for worship report having difficulty in saying 'who' or even ' what' for them is the object of worship. Sometimes one logical consequence of such difficulty is hesitation about the use of the word 'worship' at all. For some the difficulty is described as 'not finding the words': for others it is recognised as a lack of first-hand experience, or simply of 'faith'.

Yet there seems to be more agreement about the value placed by members and attenders on this one corporate act — the meeting for worship — than on any other activity or attribute of our Society. Here we meet another and baffling paradox. Many Friends who feel quite unable with integrity to report any personal sense of God's spirit or guidance in their daily lives — and consequently to pray — continue at the same time to remain among those able to assert that God is both present in our ordinary meetings for worship, and ready and able to guide us in seeking and reaching our decisions during meetings for worship for business. How is this symptom to be interpreted?

If any group of people come together for what can fairly be called a religious as distinct from a secular purpose, it must have some religious frame of reference to give it an identity. For most of their history until very recently, the frame of reference for Quakers could be clearly stated: the *shared first-hand spiritual experience of Quakers*, both inwardly as individuals and collectively in the meeting for worship. Such first-hand experience was generally understood, though variously named, as the activity of God's spirit, addressed to the reality of our present condition. The widespread inability to report such personal spiritual experience must therefore be seen as a potentially crucial symptom of our corporate dis-ease.

And what about 'faith', just mentioned above? For Quakers faith has never been anything like a 'package of beliefs', but the word does imply 'belief'. So while there can be no answer to the question ' What do Quakers believe?', it is reasonable to expect that most individual Quakers could on request provide some sort of answer to the question 'What do *you believe*?', or at least to report where they are so far on their personal 'pilgrimage of faith'. Increasingly they seem to find this difficult or impossible — and not always because 'they cannot find the words' in a situation where traditional religious language has become ambiguous or simply meaningless. Is this enough for a diagnosis? The signs and symptoms listed above are essentially factual. The interpretation placed upon them must of necessity be subjective, but that cannot be a good reason for ignoring them. We should not forget the signs of health-seeking noted earlier, or current evidence of widespread awareness, on the part of an active minority of members, that all is not well, and these should be viewed in a positive light.

Our local meetings

The role of our local meetings in enabling a positive response to our present situation depends on the way in which they perceive themselves, and then on the validity of that perception. So I must ask right away whether they see themselves as communities, and if so, what kind of community. Once again, I face the risk of ill-founded generalisation, so I will approach this question of community by setting out one picture which may accurately describe some, perhaps many, of our local meetings.

In what sense is it meaningful to think of a Quaker meeting as an actual or a potential community? And what is, or could be, its interactive relationship with the wider, looser quasi-communities of neighbourhood, township or city?

Perhaps we should start by asking ourselves what it is that the members of a Quaker meeting are aware of having in common, what it is that they share. This is, as the old saying goes, where the fun begins ! Yes — we can usually depend on an early reference to the central importance of the meeting for worship. An emphasis on 'caring for one another' may well come next. Soon after that there will be reference to a variety— perhaps a great variety — of matters that members of the meeting are concerned about — such as peace, racism, sexism, the criminal justice system to name but a few. But in these social concerns individual Friends are quite likely to be involved in or with organizations having no Quaker basis or other connections.

Some meetings may have embarked, as meetings, on projects which serve their neighbourhood or town in specific ways, and which involve a significant number of members and attenders. To what extent do any of these activities, singly or in combination, form a Quaker meeting into a community? The meeting for worship apart, is the Quaker meeting any more or less of a 'community' than is, for example, a Rotary Club? Or — everything else apart — is it the meeting for worship alone that is thought to make it a community?

There are many Quaker meetings in which the members value the silence, but perceive its purpose very differently; enjoy one another's company but do not form a community of faith; practise consensus democracy rather than seeking God's will and guidance together; and display a heartwarming readiness to be tolerant, both of this diversity and of the meeting's inability to meet their deepest spiritual needs. We must face the possibility that very few Quaker meetings can fairly be described as 'communities', simply because most lack, both in *depth and in breadth*, the essential elements to justify the description, and consequently are unable to behave as communities.

It is my lively hope that many of you will be in a position to respond to this by saying, in truth and with conviction, 'We do not recognize this picture of our condition, for it simply does not apply in our case'. Yes — where enough individual members find sufficient common ground in *the personal faith* that is *expressed in their lives*, and *shared with one another at a deep level*, a 'community of faith' will come into being. So you might well continue 'The great diversity among us in our individual religious convictions we welcome as a source of strength, and we do not experience it as a strain upon our unity. Although the ways in which we express our faith in God are different, it is nevertheless *a faith based upon our first-hand experience* which we have learned to share with one another as a group — in worship, in study, in retreat and in action. We are indeed a community of faith, and we can and do witness to the power and leading of God's Spirit in our lives— as individuals, as households and as a meeting.'

To this my response could only be one of joy and thanksgiving, not least because you would be making clear that a secular trend is not characteristic of your meeting. I am glad to record that I know of such meetings, but still wonder how many other meetings are in a position to echo your words. In the 1998 report[24] of a study of 'learning and nurture in Britain Yearly Meeting', the author noted that:

41

> 'It was this lack of a sense of spiritual fellowship which came out as the greatest need, felt by Friends across the country.'

And in this connection she cited the following comments from respondents:

> 'My meeting is inadequate theologically and politically. It certainly isn't a safe space to talk about spirituality.'

> 'I wish we were favoured by an inspiring individual or two. We can't expect a Christ in every meeting, but a John the Baptist would be nice.'

> 'Much as I appreciate my fellow-members' contribution to the life of our small PM, we have become a cosy club, instead of a group exploring union with God.'

While we must recognise thankfully the sheer amount of *caring* that is going on, we need also to give thought to the cost of this in terms of time and human loving. Pastoral care on this scale is more dependent on the *availability of spiritual nurture, for both the carers and the cared-for*, than seems generally to be realised. The provision of such spiritual nurture within a religious society without a paid clergy has until recently been seen as one of the principal ministries of eldership. But the supply of such eldership has depended on the breadth and depth of the first-hand spiritual experience of many members of each meeting: when this lessens significantly, not only does the supply dry up, but the channels for the Holy Spirit as guide and Comforter gradually become narrower, and eventually cease to be open. It is one thing to have many of our members uncertain about the present reality of our Christian heritage, but quite another when we must go further, to wonder whether we are gradually becoming a very friendly society, rather than a religious one. Perhaps those who think that God's purposes may not include a continuing role for such an increasingly diverse handful of highly individualistic 'Quakers' are right.

Overview: our corporate integrity

In his *Varieties of religious experience*[25], William James provided us with a bench mark when he wrote:

> 'The Quaker religion which Fox founded is something which it is impossible to over praise. In a day of shams it was a religion of veracity rooted in spiritual inwardness, and a return to something more like the original Gospel truth than men (sic) had ever known in England.'

It is time to say plainly, despite the signs of fresh openness engendered by the 1994 response to the draft revision, that again the gulf between theory and practice is sufficiently wide to demand a renewed faithfulness from this generation of British Quakers. It must be said that we have created the conditions for our corporate integrity in spiritual matters to be called in question. What was a Religious Society has largely become a friendly society, in which many people feel at home because they find us welcoming, tolerant and caring. Once outside the treasured Sunday morning meeting for worship, we often go through the motions, most notably in what we still claim to be our 'meetings for worship for business'.

We know perfectly well that many of our fellow-Quakers feel uncomfortable with 'Christ-language', others with 'God language' as well, some with religious language generally. But it is not only a matter of language: *it goes far deeper than that — to our collective failure to challenge and to help one another to become finders* in the spiritual life, instead of perpetual seekers. In one article[26] published in *The Friend*, the writer noted:

> '...*early Quakers seemed to have a strong spiritual life, something very powerful going on inside them that changed lives and could change society. What was it? I wanted that transforming joy that early Quakers were willing to pay for with their lives. What was their discipline of seeking — and more important, of finding?*'

In any honest attempt to answer sincere questions about the perceived 'diversity' of creed-less Quakers, integrity now demands frank admission that we are a mixture holding atheistic, agnostic, humanist, Unitarian and Quaker Christian positions, to name only the main components. Until we are a great deal more honest and courageous, among ourselves as well as in the wider world, and face up to the painful fact that corporately we too frequently go through the motions of our religious testimonies, we are to that extent what William James described as a 'sham' rather than a 'religion of veracity rooted in spiritual inwardness'. But I have been impelled to attempt this essay because I continue to hope that we may still be given an opportunity to be serviceable. For that to be reasonable, then to what ministry of divine healing and spiritual renewal must we become willing to entrust ourselves? For if anything at all can be said to be obvious, it is the impossibility of writing out a human prescription. The condition is basically spiritual, and the crucial determinants of recovery are the attitudes and readiness to cooperate of the patient.

For us to arrive at a positive description of our yearly meeting enjoying 'vigorous spiritual health', the starting point must be an admission of the need for change. And that would entail both open-ness and a re-ordering of priorities for the use of our disposable time.

As Joan Fitch concluded ten years ago:

> *'We all need to seek renewal, first and foremost in our own spiritual life, and then extraordinary things may begin to happen towards the establishment of the Kingdom.'*

It would demand faith, the placing of trust, in the love and the wisdom of God the healer. That requires the degree of individual and communal humility which Jesus required of Nicodemus, stated in terms of 're-birth' that he did not understand. Will our small British part of the Religious Society of Friends in the Truth understand, if the only remedy God can offer is that it be born again?

Or is our 'Christian heritage' now so secularised that we are really humanists at heart? If the answer for many British Quakers has in all honesty to be 'Yes', their integrity must lovingly be respected. But for the rest of us the time has come to avow our discipleship, and to face the consequences. We shall not be risking crucifixion, or imprisonment or any other physical penalty. We are only asked to 'appear foolish to the Greeks' in contemporary terms, to make public our private faith, to say where we stand. Silence is our basis for worship, not a haven for the fainthearted.

If this summary can be shown to be seriously mistaken or exaggerated, I shall be the most chastened and relieved Quaker for many miles around. For the moment I shall assume that it is not. If we are prepared to be 'open to the

Light, open to the life', we shall not like everything that we are shown. There is a very real possibility that many of us will become defensive, both personally and on behalf of our meeting and of the Society. I must hope that we shall be humble and resilient, able to face the facts of our situation.

IV

This last section will as far as possible be positive; I am very conscious that what has gone before may have seemed too gloomy, to have ignored the brighter side completely. It probably did: this was meant to be, and is, a short essay. In previous Quaker writing, at much greater length, I have tried to strike a proper balance[28]. My present endeavour is to enlist the interest and support of my fellow-Quakers and active Attenders in stemming a slow thirty-year drift towards a humanist or secular Quaker identity, from a religious society to a friendly society.

The yearly meeting as an action source

In our yearly meeting there are several places where positive action can be initiated. The actual occasion of Yearly Meeting, whether in London or residentially elsewhere, is sometimes one of them. The programme has however been decided on the advice of the Yearly Meeting Agenda Committee, and the greater flexibility of recent times is entrusted during the proceedings to the Arrangements Committee. The 'inspirational address' has almost become a thing of the past, with the result that the Swarthmore Lecture — not part of the Yearly Meeting at all — tends to fulfil that function. Those selected by the Agenda Committee to introduce sessions are strictly limited to a few minutes. That increases the time available for the subject to be before the meeting, but at a price.

The Yearly Meeting Agenda Committee is the filter through which issues raised by monthly meetings and by central committees must pass. For all practical purposes it decides which of them come before the yearly meeting in session, and in what way. I can gladly testify to the joy and privilege of serving on this committee, the only one that I have felt almost bereaved to leave at the end of the customary maximum of six years. It can be depended upon to do its work as a meeting for worship, often spontaneously falling silent as the search to cooperate with God's purposes continues. So yes, positive action to meet a perceived need can be initiated by the yearly meeting as it responds in its sessions to the topics laid before it by its Agenda Committee.

It remains to be seen whether those participating in the 1999 Yearly Meeting are challenged as well as nurtured by the 'guided worship sessions' each morning, and by a full session on 'trusting our discernment'. As already noted (p. 23) the Agenda Committee expressed the hope that 'Friends will share their experiences of discernment, and what being a Quaker means, and take back to their meetings a supportive sense of belonging to Britain Yearly Meeting.' Mention has just been made of the central committees as sources of initiatives. For the concern which is the basis of this essay, the most relevant of those committees is that of Quaker Home Service, the task of which (as stated in *Quaker faith and practice* 8.07) is–

> 'to support and strengthen the life of local meetings, the individuals within them and the yearly meeting as a whole. The ultimate strength of the Society rests to a considerable degree on the **quality of spiritual life** and pastoral care in its local meetings, and their ability to reach out and welcome enquirers.' (**My emphasis**)

From the minutes quoted on page 20, we can see at once that this responsibility for the 'quality of spiritual life' has been firmly accepted by both Quaker Home Service Central Committee, and its Committee on Eldership and Oversight. These initiatives leave me as a member of Britain Yearly

Meeting with a feeling of deep gratitude for this evidence of faithfulness.

But it is necessary to say clearly that deep-seated and lasting *spiritual* change cannot be achieved solely or even mainly through decisions taken by the Yearly Meeting in session; nor through the deliberations of Meeting for Sufferings; nor by action on the part of Quaker Home Service, or any other central body. It is neither a policy nor an administrative process, and the role of QHS must be to respond, to stimulate, to enable, and to nurture. (That assertion begs the question, unless I add '... and is enabled to do so through *budgetary recognition that the work of Quaker Home Service calls for top priority in the allocation of limited central funds').

Further, what has been called 'constitutional change' should not be attempted until particular areas of such change have been identified as *essential to facilitate perceived upward movements of spiritual renewal.*

The monthly meetings

Logically, we should now consider the role of our 73 monthly meetings. Individual membership is held in them, not locally; they are the recognised channels through which nearly all Quaker business from the 'grassroots' must pass to reach Meeting for Sufferings, the Yearly Meeting Agenda Committee, and the central committees. Against that background of responsibility it is disturbing to the point of becoming bizarre that most of them are unrepresentative, through poor attendance, of the membership of their constituent local meetings. In a 1993 study[28] involving personal visits to the clerks of 55 of our monthly meetings, it was found that attendance averaged only 14 per cent of the listed members, varying from a 'low' of 5 per cent to an exceptional 'high' of 46 per cent. It is clear from that report that none of the clerks interviewed felt able to suggest new ways of improving attendance at business meetings. For our present purposes, I shall accept that finding, and recognise that this problem of participation in monthly meeting business can only be addressed at the level of the individual member. Just as an individual cannot progress, morally or spiritually, without recognition and admission of failure, of 'missing the mark' ('conviction/convincement'), and of being in need of grace if change is to start ('conversion'), so will the British part of our 'beloved Society' fail to move forward as the Religious Society it still claims to be. But fresh convincement, and progressive conversion, of the whole body depends upon each one of us, at whatever point we have reached in our seeking, being 'open to the Light', to being 'convicted' by the Spirit.

At the personal level

Before presuming to challenge others, I must be open myself. Neither age nor length of membership can justify my engaging in what 17th and 18th century Quakers would not have hesitated to call preaching. I am not a 'recorded minister', as were most of the preachers in those days; I am without credentials. So you are entitled to know where my words come from, and then to judge for yourself.

Several times in the last ten years, I have pleaded for general reluctance to use labels to describe groups of people. I would not, for example, ever refer to 'the disabled' or to 'the mentally ill'. So amongst Quakers I regret the use of labels such as 'Christocentric' or 'Universalist', more especially because such use inevitably has become divisive. But during the last five years, I have along with some other

British Quakers become convinced that this polarisation is not our basic problem, though preoccupation with it can prevent people from recognising that many Quakers see themselves as both Quaker Christians and universalists. In so doing, they are but emulating Fox, Penn or Woolman.

I am one of those, and in an evening address at Warwick in 1993 set out my religious position as follows:–

> *"Faith" for me is not a package of beliefs: it is a matter of where I place my ultimate trust. When asked to say where I have reached so far in my spiritual development, I can with confidence based on experience describe myself as a believer in the same "Christ" who spoke to Fox's condition. And if asked to explain what that means to me, I find it difficult to better the answer given by Justin Martyr in the second century CE, as paraphrased by Henry Chadwick:–*
>
>> *"Justin argues that the light that all men (*sic*) have is implanted by the divine Reason, the Logos of God who was incarnate in Jesus, and who is* **universally** *active and present in the highest goodness and intelligence* **wherever they may be found***. The divine Logos inspired the prophets, he says, and was present entire in Jesus Christ. '.* (**My emphasis**) –

That is why I must break my own rule — to identify myself as a Quaker Christian universalist, who trusts God, is 'saved' from my wilfulness by the Inward Light of Christ, knows that the Holy Spirit is ready to guide and to enable, if I will but attend expectantly and go as I am led.

Every one of us is on a journey — through this mortal life. We are also on a spiritual journey, whether we know it or not, whether we admit it or not, whether we like it or not. The vast majority of our members and active attenders readily claim to be 'seekers': but if one does not know what one is looking for, any search is bound to be fruitless. That is probably the principal reason why so few Quakers are able, on request from enquirers and attenders, to say what they have found so far.

Among those of us who *do* know what we are seeking, the reluctance to report our findings may often arise from our doubts. Listen then to Gerard Hughes, in the opening lines of the Preface to his book *God of surprises* [29].

> *'I am a Catholic, a priest, and a Jesuit. Many people still think that Catholic priests, perhaps Jesuits especially, never suffer confusion, bewilderment or disillusion. I do.'*

So do I.

So did Thomas Merton, the Trappist monk recognised as one of the spiritual giants of this century. Shortly before his untimely death on his Asian journey in 1968, he wrote in his journal:

> *'Faith means doubt. Faith is not the suppression of doubt. It is the overcoming of doubt, and you overcome doubt by going through it. The man of faith who has not experienced doubt is not a man of faith.'*[30]

This is the reality within which we are challenged to pursue our search. And for what are we searching? I dare not speak for others, but for myself I can say 'I seek to let God enable me to become the man God knows about'. In other words, I am seeking to realise my true identity, as one known and loved by God. To make that possible, I had to accept that I had 'missed the mark' — the original meaning of the term 'sinned' — and 'repent' that I had done so. Then, as a 20th-century man, I was amazed to find for myself what Fox, my 17th-century predecessor, had found — that there was one who spoke to my condition. And I soon realised that to be only the beginning of a life-long spiritual journey,[31] the journey of conversion — of sustained readiness to admit failure and to start again, over and over again, to be changed from within by the power of the divine Spirit.

That is my testimony, Friends. If it helps you to define the object of your seeking, but in your own words not mine, I shall rejoice. If you already know your target, and my testimony encourages you to persevere and to become ready to share your findings, I shall rejoice with you.

I hope that by now it will be obvious that my concern for Quakers in Britain is not limited by distinctions between 'Christian' and any other belief system to which individual Quakers may have been attracted, whether before or after coming into membership of the Society through their monthly meeting. My concern is to assert afresh that ours is a religious society, not a secular or humanist one; that we are therefore called individually and corporately to a constant renewal of spiritual experience; and that on the basis of such personal experience we shall be equipped joyfully to offer our thousands of seeking Attenders *something to which they will wish to commit themselves —* despite commitment being out-of fashion in our pre-millennial culture.

In my abstention from a narrow emphasis upon our heritage of a distinctive form of Christianity, I am not simply being tolerant, broad-minded, inclusive — which I hope I am: I am also being realistic in my recognition that probably only a minority of the active membership of Britain Yearly Meeting would be prepared to describe themselves as 'Quaker Christians'. To the majority, I can say gladly that so long as they are engaged on a spiritual search, and share with me my concern to stem the tide of secularism now evident, I shall 'count them in'. Having done so, however, I address my call for a renewal of personal spiritual experience to both those groups of my fellow-members.

To those of my fellow-Quakers who do perceive themselves as Quaker Christians, and who may be dismayed by what I have just written, I have this to say: the initiative always rests with God. If by the action of God's Spirit more of our fellow Quakers and future members are brought to the point of seeing themselves as Quaker Christians, and as a result Britain Yearly Meeting can rightly claim to be part of the Church universal, then to God be the praise. But we must always remember that Jesus is reported as saying 'In my father's house there are many mansions', and as not hesitating to include the despised Samaritans.

That said, I must call again on the insight of Thomas Merton, when he observed somewhere that one can only fully respect the deeply-held faith of another when one is rooted and grounded in one's own. It was on that basis that shortly before his death in 1968, he met on terms of equality and friendship with the Dalai Llama. Somewhere in here there is a vital question of integrity, to which we Quakers assert ourselves committed. It permits no one, whatever their personal beliefs or lack of belief to be, in a loose modern sense, 'all things to all men'.

We should speak lovingly to the differing conditions of those we meet from where we are ourselves. The challenge is to be spiritually adventurous — to discard our prejudices and to look at this central Quaker principle of 'the Light' as if it was a novel experience. When we do that, it may not be long before simple honesty compels us to admit that we have never thought of it in quite that way before. The 'light' we are accustomed to reading and talking about these days in most Quaker circles is vague, abstract and usually warm and comfortable. If indeed we can affirm it to be something to do with God, then it is the 'loving' attributes of God which we have in mind — conveniently forgetting that these must often involve some chastening. And modern liberal Quakers never talk about 'sin' — of which the Inward Light might convince us if we admitted its existence.

Time

Even those unfamiliar with the New Testament are likely to have heard about the dire warning 'Where your treasure is there will your heart be also'. This is a basic truth about human motivation, and still to be heeded. But we can use the idea of 'treasure' more broadly to give us an additional criterion. What about 'As you use your time, so can your loyalties be seen' ? Yes — but we must qualify this, and consider whatever proportion of our waking hours is normally at our disposal, to use as we think fit.

We are all aware that for people in Britain who are in full time employment, disposable time has been drastically reduced as compared with even a decade ago. For the majority, this reduction is caused by the now well-established practice of what in effect is compulsory overtime. Many companies use this as an alternative to recruiting more workers. For those on salaries, pressure at the workplace can mean working more hours there, or taking work home — or both.

Part-time work accounts for a high proportion of the 'new jobs' reported in the employment statistics. Most part-time workers are women, who if they are parents will often find that they have little time 'to call their own'. The situation will be even more difficult if they are single parents, or if their husbands are prevented by their own job-demands from sharing the domestic load. And yes — there are husbands who could take their share, but fail to pull their weight.

All that is but recognition that most people face limits on their disposable time: they do not enjoy the luxury of a fully-retired Quaker of eighty-odd years. But whatever the amount of your disposable time, however little, *there is enough*. The first step for you may be to find just enough time — alone and quiet — to *let God tell you how to use your time*. The self-discipline of one's religious life is largely a matter of being practical.

Priorities

It is against such a background of realism that I must put forward a challenge to us all:

> *The solution can only be found through change in the lives of each one of us.*

Such change can only come on a voluntary basis: no one is going to compel it, there is no place for coercion. But there are prerequisites to be met, and it may be helpful as well as salutary to set them out plainly. Modern British Quakers tend to recoil from any suggestion of discipline, even when it is consists of freely-chosen self-discipline. And however much they may approve Whittier's line 'May our ordered lives confess the beauty of Thy peace', they continue without the order, while yearning for the peace.

The most revered Quaker document of this century, *A testament of devotion*,[32] contains Thomas Kelly's prescription:

> 'Much of our acceptance of multitudes of obligations is due to our inability to say "no"... When we say "yes" or "no" on the basis of heady decisions, we have to give reasons, to ourselves and to others. But when we say "yes" or "no" to calls on the basis of inner guidance and whispered promptings from the Centre of our life ... we have no reason to give but one — the will of God as we discern it. Then we have begun to live in guidance.'

Please read that again.

So our first step towards gaining some spiritual depth is to ask ourselves 'What is the Centre of my life?' Does that provide us with a new way of thinking about our faith? For myself, my faith consists of placing my trust in God, when the deepest issues of my existence, my identity and my ultimate worth are at stake. This involves acceptance of God as God is, and of myself as I am, without endless questioning that only erects barriers.

On that basis, I seek to keep God as the Centre of my life. But with Thomas Kelly, 'I should like to be mercilessly drastic in uncovering any sham pretence of being wholly devoted to the inner holy Presence, in singleness of love to God.'

An American Quaker once observed to me 'The worst enemy of the spiritual life is the pocket diary'. Does that ring a bell with you, Friend? Are you so frantically busy that you leave little or none of your disposable time for the self-discipline of daily 'listening' to the nudgings of the

Spirit? Within whatever time there is, does the priority go to the Centre, to being open to 'inner guidance and whispered promptings'?

Living on such a basis is much easier when shared. If that is not possible at home, is it possible in your local Quaker meeting? Can you think of anyone with whom you worship on Sunday mornings who might enter into a mutually-rewarding fellowship of listening to the Spirit? Or do you have a friend outside your Quaker circle who might do so?

And if you come to the conclusion that there is probably no one in the meeting likely to respond positively, what are the implications? Perhaps it simply reflects the well-known tendency, mentioned by many attenders, for Quakers to be reticent about their spiritual findings on their individual seeking journeys. As a result, you simply may not be aware that one or more people in your meeting might in fact be approachable and receptive.

But it may mean more than that, it may be an indication of need for 'inreach'. Perhaps you could put a notice in the newsletter, inviting those interested to meet with you for a preliminary discussion.

And you could ask the convenor of your meeting's group of elders about the problem. Does that group regularly hold business-free meetings, to practise listening together themselves to the nudgings of the Spirit, and to deepen its own spiritual life and fellowship? Bearing in mind what we have noted about the difficulties faced these days by many elders, be tender with them if they find your problem hard to deal with, but do not let it discourage you in your search for a solution.

It was reported recently[33] that

> 'In Norwich Meeting, and a few others, a good number of those who come to meeting on Sunday have started meetings between whiles in very small groups, two or three people only, to talk about their spiritual journey, as it is being experienced that week. "We need our journeys to be journeys, and not mere meandering around nowhere".'

This may well be one of the fruits of Rex Ambler's 'Experiment with Light', based on his four years of studying the writings of George Fox. This has been richly described in a series of three articles, published in *The Friend* during February and March 1999.[34] As the writer puts it a nutshell:

> First you stop whatever you are doing or thinking — "be still and cool in thy own mind and spirit from thy own thoughts". It helps to be still in the body too.
>
> Then, stay there, do not do anything. You will "feel the principle of God turn thy mind to the Lord God".
>
> Stay in the Light — you do not need to tell the Light what to do, or why you are there, or engage in conversation with the Light, you just wait.
>
> That's it. When you wait in the Light, the Light shows you whatever you need to see. It will change you, rebuke you, heal you, give you life — whatever is right for you.'

To live spiritually involves the acquisition of a skill, and its honing by practice. The process can be assisted by working with an experienced teacher, whether formally or otherwise. The Quaker Retreat Group may be able to help you with this. The practice must be regular, and this demands time

— not necessarily very much — which, as we have noted, may be at a premium. Persevering, one is eventually surprised by the realisation that the skill has become 'natural', and can be exercised much of the time, not just in daily periods of quiet. Thomas Kelly called that 'living on two levels at once'.

That was a general statement about skills of all kinds. Full-timers in every domain of human activity accept and implement it, from swimmers and snooker-players to monks and nuns. Why do we think that we Quakers are different? Or is it rather a matter of values — of not making the commitment and the sustained effort because we are, after all, only part-timers in the spiritual life?

Foundations

You will have realized by now that the way forward for our local meetings only becomes evident as a few of us, individually and together in small groups, have the humility to admit our need for an active faith, a trusting of ourselves to the love of God and to the leadings of God's Spirit in our daily lives. The way forward for our meeting depends on some of its members freely choosing to accept a discipline of the spiritual life, both in solitude and in community. Growth in the spiritual life will then be wholly dependent on our continuing readiness to let God show us what are the right priorities for the use of our gifts, our resources, and — most critically — our time. It will be dependent on our disciplined alertness day by day, so that we become aware that even previously right priorities have been changed. We need from time to time to ask God 'Is this task you laid upon me last year still what you want me to be doing, or do you now have other priorities for me ?'
How easy it is to complain that there is too much coming

'topdown' from 'the centre', and too little coming up from 'the grassroots'? Dear reader, we — not the preparative or the monthly meeting — we the men and women in our local meetings *are* the grassroots!

If you and I do not choose to open ourselves to the Light, if we are secretly afraid of being inwardly challenged, and enabled to change, the religious life of our local meetings, our monthly meetings, our yearly meeting will remain at risk. Only through our individual courage, our self-discipline and our faithfulness can the drift from 'religious society' to 'friendly society' be checked and reversed. As William Penn and other Quakers since have said:

'There is no time but this present.'

References

1. Part of a minute of York Monthly Meeting, 1859.
2. **John Stephenson ROWNTREE**, *Quakerism past and present*. London: Smith Elder 1859.
3. **Alastair HERON**, *Quakers in Britain: a century of change 1895-1995*. Kelso: Curlew Productions 1995.
4. **John PUNSHON**, *Portrait in grey: a short history of the Quakers*. London: Quaker Home Service 1984.
5. *Quaker faith and practice*. London: Britain Yearly Meeting 1995.
6. 'The Tabular Statement for 1998', from *Documents in advance* for Yearly Meeting 1999.
7. *Documents in advance* for Yearly Meeting 1998.
8. **Joan FITCH**, *The present tense: talking to our time*. Birmingham: Woodbrooke College 1980.
9. *Quakers in Britain* [see 3 above].
10. **Christine TREVETT**, *Previous convictions*. London: Quaker Home Service 1997.
11. **John PUNSHON**, *Testimony and tradition*. London: Quaker Home Service 1990.
12. **Margaret HEATHFIELD**, *Being together*. London: Quaker Home Service 1994.
13. **Alastair HERON**, *Now we are Quakers*. York: Quaker Outreach in Yorkshire 1994.
14. "How has the Quaker pie been changing?" Pie-charts based on the 'Tabular Statement 1977- 1997.' [compiled by MBS 20.8.98].
15. *Needs of our elders and overseers*. YM Elders & Overseers Executives 1988.
16. *Now we are Quakers* [see 13 above].
17. **Elisabeth ALLEY**, *Patterns of giving: a survey of Friends' interests and commitments beyond the Schedule*. York: the author 1998.
18. *Quakers in Britain* [see 3 above].

19. **Keith REDFERN**, *What are our monthly meetings doing?* London: Quaker Home Service 1993.

20. *The nature and variety of concern.* London: Quaker Home Service (for Meeting for Sufferings) 1992.

21. *To Lima with love.* London: Quaker Home Service 1987.

22. **Alastair HERON**, *QuakerSpeak.* York: Quaker Outreach in Yorkshire [2nd edit.] 1997.

23. *What do you do in Meeting for Worship?* Statements by Members and Attenders of Newcastle-upon-Tyne PM 1989.

24. **Peggy HEEKS**, *Growing in the Spirit: learning and nurture in Britain Yearly Meeting,* York: Joseph Rowntree Charitable Trust 1998.

25. **William JAMES**, *The varieties of religious experience.* London 1902.

26. **Anne HOSKING**, 'Longing for the Light', *The Friend* 5 February 1999, p. 10.

27. *Quakers in Britain* [see 3 above].

28. **Keith REDFERN** [see 19 above].

29. **Gerard W. HUGHES**, *God of surprises.* London: Darton, Longman and Todd 1985.

30. **Thomas MERTON**, *The Asian Journal* (Appendix iii). Sheldon Press 1974.

31. **Alastair HERON**, *Only one life: a Quaker's voyage.* Kelso: Curlew Productions 1998.

32. **Thomas R. KELLY**, *A testament of devotion* (1941) London: Quaker Home Service [1979 edition].

33. **Rachel BRITTON**, 'Religious experience'. *Quaker Monthly* Vol. 78-2, February 1999. p. 27.

34. **Anne HOSKING**, 'Longing for the Light'; Experimenting with Light'; 'A meditation on Light'. *The Friend* 5 and 19 February, 5 March 1999.

Publications in print, by the same author

Obtainable from:
Quaker Bookshop, Friends House, Euston Rd, London NW1 2BJ

Caring, conviction, commitment: dilemmas of Quaker membership today (83 pp) Quaker Home Service and Woodbrooke College 1992. Based on a survey of the experiences and views of 459 Attenders across Yorkshire General Meeting.

Gifts and ministries [2nd (revised) edition] (22 pp). Quaker Home Service 1993. A discussion paper on eldership.

Now we are Quakers: the experience and views of new members (64 pp). Quaker Outreach in Yorkshire 1994. The experiences and views of 200 men and women, across the whole yearly meeting, who became Members during the year 1992.

QuakerSpeak: first aid for newcomers [2nd (revised) edition] (55 pp) Quaker Outreach in Yorkshire 1994, 1997, 1999 A pocket-sized guide to Quaker acronyms, terms and expressions, committees and other bodies in Britain Yearly Meeting.

Obtainable from:
Curlew Productions, Thirlestane House, Kelso TD5 8PD

Quakers in Britain; a century of change 1895-1995 (176 pp) Curlew Productions 1995. The only major publication to mark the centenary of the 1895 Manchester Conference, and to provide an evaluative study of the following 100 years.

The British Quakers 1647-1997 (44 pp) Curlew Productions 1997. This slim economical volume, abstracted from ***Quakers in Britain***, is intended mainly for enquirers, attenders and new members.

Only one life: a Quaker's voyage (164 pp) Curlew Productions 1998. [illustrated autobiography, 1915-1998].